Solved
in 7

Please read this book. If you enjoy it, please support a local indie author by posting on social media and sharing the book with someone else.

www.solvedin7.com

The Power of
Disciplined
Problem-Solving

Solved in 7

Jim Sholler

Copyright © 2022 Jim Sholler

All rights reserved.

Solved in 7

The Power of Disciplined Problem-Solving

ISBN 978-1-5445-3003-1 Hardcover
       978-1-5445-3004-8 Paperback
       978-1-5445-3005-5 Ebook

To my wife, Kim,

and my daughters, Jessie and Courtney,

who inspire, encourage, and

tolerate me

Contents

Introduction

In just 7 minutes, I solved a problem the best doctors in New York and Boston had been unable to solve for over thirteen years. The doctors experimented, tried to prove theories, burned through millions of insurance dollars, and ultimately pointed fingers at the patient who happened to be my wife. None of her doctors embraced or even attempted disciplined problem-solving. Once a disciplined framework was used, the problem was diagnosed in 7 minutes. I'm not a doctor, and I have no medical background, but difficult problems don't care about your background, area of expertise, or how long the issue has persisted. Fortunately, the right methodology transcends the variables of different problems. Anyone who can apply the proper problem-solving framework correctly can connect the dots and solve previously intractable problems. I'm here to share that framework with you. And let's face it, in this world, we all have problems.

Life is a series of transitions from one problem to the next. The sequence only ends with the ultimate unsolvable problem: physical mortality. Problems are pervasive in every aspect of our lives. Companies and individuals are dying a slow death (in some cases, literally, like my wife) because people are not trained how to solve problems efficiently and effectively. I consider myself fortunate to be passionate about solving problems, and I can tell you from experience that there is a better way. What is the most difficult problem in your life right now? You may be facing a multi-year monster of a problem like I was previously. It may seem like a bottomless pit, because difficult problems have a way of appearing impossible to solve. Perhaps you want to improve the culture, productivity, and effectiveness of your company. Perhaps you want to help someone else you know or love to learn the answers to a challenging problem.

There is no guarantee that you can solve all problems quickly. Still, if you commit to the disciplined use of this framework and engage the right Subject Matter Experts (SMEs, pronounced "smees"), you will, on average, significantly reduce the time you require to resolve problems. This framework is your secret weapon. You will learn how to solve challenging problems that have no known solution. You will learn how to recognize and avoid the typical behaviors that conspire against discovering the answers you need. No one needs a person who thinks they have all the answers, but everyone needs the person who can help them learn the answers. You will be that person.

I can assure you that most any problem is solvable when the right experts are participating in a well-managed learning process that eliminates the typical bad behaviors associated with challenging problems. I cannot promise you'll be completely past whatever the issue is, but, just as I did, it's quite possible you'll turn the corner and make progress. And you'll likely be able to do so in an astonishingly short time frame.

Whether you are facing a difficult problem at work or in your personal life, this book can help. You will learn the 7 simple steps to frame the problem, manage SMEs through the iterative process (including how to document facts and generate proper questions), and identify and eliminate ineffective behaviors from the process. The term "problem" has a broad spectrum of definitions ranging from unwanted situations or matters that are difficult to solve to people who are difficult to deal with. For the purposes of this book, problems are things that are broken or present unexpected behavior. Consider "things" to be processes, functions, or mechanical objects. As you will see in the examples provided in this book, we encounter broken processes, functions, and mechanical objects in our personal and professional lives on a daily basis. There are very few skills a person can learn that position them to meet the inexhaustible demand for their services throughout life; effectively solving problems is one of these universally applicable skills.

Humans, in general, have the raw cognitive ability to assess, categorize, and either resolve or avoid problems. With that said, the ability to do so efficiently and effectively requires training and practice. Despite the existence of many problem-solving methodologies, standard educational models do not address problem-solving skills. Most large corporations also neglect to train talent in problem-solving skills. People are left to rely on their natural, undisciplined tendencies to solve problems. Many individuals receive training, but the lack of relatable, memorable examples during that training results in those individuals returning to undisciplined behavior soon after. This book provides a clear, proven framework and a series of compelling stories that will resonate with you and motivate you to employ the lessons learned. Empowering more people to use this framework will also foster a culture of problem-solving for your organization, and the framework's approach will become second nature if you are genuinely disciplined about using it. You will also find that you have differentiated yourself from your peers, elevated your brand, and acquired the necessary tools to navigate challenging personal problems as well.

Every problem does not require the use of a problem-solving framework. For example, when the first problem of your day is that you run out of toothpaste, you do not need a practiced methodology to assess the root cause. From a lifetime of brushing your teeth, you instinctively know that the tube is empty because you used 100 percent of the contents. You also know the mitigating action: get more toothpaste. In some cases, the problem may be more complex and have multiple potential known solutions. For example, when you find that you have a flat tire in the morning, you immediately know your options include:

- Calling a service to repair the tire

- Adding air so you can drive to a repair service

- Taking a car service instead of driving

- Simply changing your plans to delay the urgency

In this scenario, you may be less concerned about the root cause than simply mitigating the impact. You already know how to fix the underlying problem by replacing or repairing the tire. Unlike this example, a problem that requires disciplined problem-solving is one for which a solution is not already known.

The Solved In 7 framework can be applied across a broad spectrum of professional and personal problems with seemingly no known resolution. You will learn how to recognize four ineffective methods commonly implemented by people facing problems. You will then see a series of examples where these behaviors hindered the learning process and how the framework subsequently helped resolve each problem. The framework enabled the resolution of each one in under 7 minutes in most cases. The final example is my wife's medical story, which demonstrates all of the medical establishment's ineffective behaviors spanning many years until my framework facilitated solving the problem in under 7 minutes. The intent of these examples is to help you recognize your own ineffective behaviors and replace them with my powerful framework to solve any problem at work or home.

I'm passionate about sharing the framework and providing problem resolution services via SolvedIn7.com, because I know there's an infinite number of unsolved problems that haven't been addressed efficiently or effectively. Companies are wasting resources and thousands of patients are suffering, if not dying, needlessly, because people do not have the training to address these situations in a simple, structured manner. Your problems aren't solving themselves, so let me teach you how to become a problem-solving leader. Let's get started Solving in 7!

Chapter 1

How Come?

I have to give credit to my mother for being the first person to recognize my unwavering need to learn why things happen. For most of my life, she derived great pleasure in sharing that her nickname for me, when I was a child, was "Howkem." She explained that no matter what she said, I responded incessantly with "How come?" As annoying as that was, she knew my intent was sincere. I had to know why. I had to connect the dots.

Many years later, while working for Deloitte Consulting, I was assigned to a project that was already well behind schedule. We were attempting to organize software for a major client who experienced significant computer system issues. I was extremely frustrated that no one could provide me with an inventory of all software or an overview of the process we were utilizing to work our way through the pile. I quietly pulled my own inventory and tracking process together because I needed more information to understand the magnitude of the problem and how long it would take to finish. That inventory ultimately became the standard methodology to manage the entire project.

The project velocity accelerated, and we ultimately completed it on time with high quality. As a result, I was promoted to manager. I had mixed emotions regarding the promotion; I was proud but felt like all I did was create a spreadsheet. In actuality, this experience offered a critical early lesson in the importance of defining and following a process as a way to bring order to chaos. I love chaos because I know how good it will feel when order is restored.

My career eventually brought me to one of the largest financial institutions in the world. My commitment to bringing order to chaos was the inspiration behind my brand as "The Fixer" for the last twenty-one years of my twenty-seven-year career at this firm. I continued to employ processes to restore order and solve problems, but the processes were always unique for each situation. In 1999, while managing a team of IT engineers,

I received my first formal training in problem-solving. My manager and mentor had the foresight to pull together a comprehensive plan of attack to support our systems during the upcoming change of century from the 1900s to 2000. This change, widely referred to as Y2K, was anticipated as a potential tsunami of technology problems. The age of many mainframe systems, which were written by employees long since retired, further complicated the pending onslaught. The plan included the obvious tasks of reviewing all systems for the use of two-digit years where the preceding digits were assumed to be the number nineteen. The plan also included providing formal problem management training for all of my manager's direct reports. I attended the training with limited expectations, but I was willing to check the box. By the time I left the training, I felt like I finally had some structure to enhance what I already enjoyed doing, using well-developed processes to solve difficult problems and restore order.

I was young and already managing brilliant IT engineers, many of whom were older than I was. Consequently, I felt very self-conscious about my age and determined to demonstrate that I could add value and support my team. I wanted them to view me as more than just office furniture. I immediately applied the lessons I learned and granted myself the freedom to adapt and modify the approach as I gained experience. The approach evolved into the Solved In 7 framework. Over time my teams came to respect and need me for "that thing I do." I trained each of my teams on the framework and was asked to train other teams within our company as well.

I treated the framework as a useful trick that could increase our productivity and efficiency. After using it in this way for a few years, my confidence grew tremendously to the point where I was using it in every aspect of my life. Eventually, I used the framework to solve my wife's extremely rare bleeding disorder after the best doctors failed to do so for more than thirteen years. That was the point when I realized that the framework was more than just my little trick and that opportunities to apply it are infinite.

To understand the magnitude of the opportunity to distinguish yourself in the workplace, consider the following quote from a 2017 article by Frederik Broden in the *Harvard Business Review*:

> In surveys of 106 C-suite executives representing 91 private- and public-sector companies from 17 countries, the author found that a full 85% agreed that their organizations were bad

at problem diagnosis, and 87% agreed that this flaw carried significant costs. Fewer than one in 10 said they were unaffected by the issue.

Competition in the workplace can be fierce. Being an employee disciplined in this framework would give you an advantage at any of these companies. You would come to recognize that you achieved this advantage once people began to ask you to "do that thing you do," because they couldn't figure something out.

The survey in the article was for private- and public-sector businesses. The impact of the inability to effectively solve problems leads to financial losses, missed opportunities, erosion of reputation, and, in worst-case scenarios, product safety issues. Companies are slowly bleeding time, money, and productivity as a result of this skill gap.

Now, imagine the impact of a similar situation in the medical profession. The statistics below, from a *Healthline* article in February 2020 by Brian Mastroianni, give some perspective on the dire state of problem-solving skills in the medical profession in the U.S. as they relate to misdiagnoses:

- "In the United States, 12 million people are affected by medical diagnostic errors each year." [To put that into perspective, only six states in the U.S. have more than 12 million residents.]

- "An estimated 40,000 to 80,000 people die annually from complications from these misdiagnoses."

- "Women and minorities are 20 to 30 percent more likely to be misdiagnosed."

The need for a better way to solve problems is not only real—it's urgent. The Solved In 7 framework efficiently and accurately connects the dots in a way that is simple and repeatable.

Chapter 2

A Simple Framework

A problem-solving framework should be applicable to both professional and personal problems. The framework should be easy to explain and manage, and it should empower you to lead experts through the *learning* process. The word "learning" is emphasized here because you will *learn* the root cause instead of guessing it, or diagnosing it. Diagnosing is essentially the practice of matching known symptoms in one column to known causes in another.

Unlike diagnosing, problem-solving is the process of learning what is causing the current situation based on an analysis of facts and questions. You will manage SMEs through the learning process by assigning specific tasks and adhering to the framework. The tendency to go rogue and follow theories is ever present, so the problem resolution leader must reinforce adherence to the process and share progress with the team.

Individuals trained in this framework, as it evolved over twenty-one years, resolved each example provided in this book. This approach empowers trained resources to manage diverse experts through the learning process to resolve challenging problems. The problem resolution leaders used the framework to guide the experts through the learning process to resolve these problems in an average of 7 minutes.

Reading a book about golf without actually practicing the sport limits your growth. Similarly, knowledge of this framework without the commitment to using it will not empower you to resolve problems. The ability to lead SMEs through the problem resolution learning process comes from the consistent application of these 7 steps. No one can be a SME in everything. In most cases, the team you compile will consist of experts who possess significantly greater knowledge in critical areas than you have yourself. The team will learn about the process from you while you learn about the essential areas of expertise from them, and you will all learn the root cause of the problem together.

7-Step Framework

1. Assemble the Team

Select a limited number of SMEs who will work with you to learn the root cause of the problem. The SMEs should be individuals who meet at least one, if not all, of the following criteria:

- Expertise specific to the perceived problem

- Recent or historical knowledge of the perceived problem

- Proven track record solving similar or related problems

There is no magic number of SMEs since all problems vary in complexity and the number of interrelated components. You will need to select SMEs who can work independently. You will assign their tasks in parallel to expedite the learning process. The number of SMEs is a balance between how many you think you need, based on what you know at the start, and how many you think you can manage. You can always add more SMEs as dictated by the volume of tasks or the need for additional areas of subject matter expertise. As a rule of thumb, you should start with between one and three SMEs and supplement as needed.

2. Set Expectations with the Team

Take time to explain the learning process to the team. You are not looking for consensus concerning the learning process; you are educating the SMEs on the framework that you will employ. You want to avoid process questions that will delay the learning process.

3. State the Problem

On a team collaboration space (e.g., whiteboard or virtual collaboration tool), write a concise and focused statement that summarizes the known problem or impact as you understand it. The statement should be limited to one sentence.

> *Example*: When I turn on the kitchen faucet, no water comes out.

When formulating the problem statement, consider the process or functionality that is broken. Focus on the expected or intended result that is not working, as opposed to a current state observation. For example, in the case of a flat tire that was previously and recently flat, an accurate problem statement would be "The tire is not maintaining air pressure." The ability to maintain pressure is the broken thing. Documenting "The tire is flat again" does not reference the actual functionality—maintaining air pressure—that is broken.

Avoid the use of names or teams when writing the problem statement. Including names or teams can often lead down the path of finger-pointing. Finger-pointing is not a useful contribution to the learning process.

Also avoid documenting solution theories in the problem statement. Solution theories will be documented in a subsequent step, but they do not contribute to a clear, concise problem statement.

The problem statement is the home base of the exercise. Everyone on the team should be able to come back to the problem statement to ensure that all parties are on the same page.

Unlike Step 2, in this step you want to confirm consensus with the team. Everyone on the team must agree on exactly what the team is trying to learn.

As more facts are learned, the problem statement may be revisited and modified when appropriate to ensure that the team remains on the same page and progress continues.

4. List All Known Facts

On the left side of the team collaboration space, write "Facts" and underline it. On the right side, write "Questions" and underline it. Below "Facts," you will list all known facts. Facts are indisputable truths that someone can demonstrate repeatedly. Facts are not theories or "generally accepted" truths. Taking the time to confirm that every fact is a fact is critical. In legal terms, you cannot accept hearsay. Even a simple statement attributed to someone, such as a request to perform a task, should be confirmed in writing or from the original requester to rule out miscommunications. At the beginning of this exercise, it is helpful to specifically ask if anyone kept records of prior occurrences of the issue. If so, ensure that you have access to those records. Facts can include seemingly trivial information such as the time of day something occurred, the day of the week, the weather at that time, current call volumes, logged data, error logs, video surveillance, etc. You can never have too many facts. Once again, a consensus is critical in this step. You want to ensure that the team is in agreement that all known facts are listed. Reaffirm that learning why the problem statement is occurring remains the focus of the team. During this step, it is highly likely that questions will arise. Include all unanswered questions under the "Questions" line and continue with the collection of facts. Do not debate the answers to questions in this step; simply record them.

5. List All Known Questions

Ask the team to list any questions they can think of and record them on the right side under "Questions." Document all questions that arise. Dismissing input from team members will only keep you from the learning process, wrapped in a cloak of arrogance. Encourage the team to share all of their theories but record them in the form of questions.

> *Example*: If the team believes that this happened because another team forgot to perform a critical step, you will record, "Was step X performed by team Y at the expected time?"

Knowing what questions to ask is an acquired skill. Some individuals have excellent forensic instincts and can zero in on great questions. Some people can ask great questions based on years of subject matter expertise. Everyone else must rely on their ability to listen to generate good questions. Like trying to solve a jigsaw puzzle, you know the desired result; it's the picture on the box. In the previous kitchen faucet example, water should be coming out of the faucet. The facts and stories that people share with you are all pieces of the puzzle. One missing piece can delay or prevent the completion of the puzzle. You must listen intently for details such as what led to this point, how many other times it happened, what time it happened, etc. Team members may inadvertently withhold information, not realizing its importance. You may have no idea which pieces go where, but you know edges make up the outside and blue pieces make up the sky.

As you group pieces together, you inevitably start to see components of the bigger picture forming; the sky pieces are in one area of your table while the ground and trees are elsewhere. You will look for specific pieces to continue your progress on each of these sections.

Consider the following example: In relation to a challenging medical mystery, Rick explains that his health issue did not exist when he was visiting family in another country, so he thought the cause might be dietary, because he had been eating different foods abroad. Diet, however, is only one piece of a category we can call "potential environmental impacts." Has Rick been away from home for more than a few days at any other time, even if he remained within his home country? Were the symptoms still noticeable? How long has Rick resided at his current home location? When did Rick's symptoms first appear? Was there any recent work done on or near the house? How old is the house? Was it tested for lead or mold? Every question is one puzzle piece that might start a new section of the puzzle. Remember, you are not trying to generate theories or prove anything. You are trying to list questions and fill in the puzzle one piece at a time. It may be a cliché, but there really are no dumb questions. Eventually, the puzzle will be complete, and the picture will present itself.

6. Assign Questions to Each SME Accordingly

Assign the questions to the SMEs and reemphasize that they are not proving theories; they are answering questions and learning new facts. Instruct the SMEs to let you know if they require any additional resources to obtain the necessary facts.

Ask the team to report back immediately as they learn new facts. Do not wait for a scheduled meeting as this may waste time if one of the SMEs uncovers a critical fact. You will list all new facts on the team collaboration space so team members can view the current state of knowledge at any moment.

7. Rinse and Repeat

You will pull the team back together when they answer all of the questions. Document each new fact and then reassess the problem statement (Step 3) and reaffirm the consensus. (On a side note, there are occasions where the answer to a single question presents the root cause of the problem. When that occurs, continuing to research the remaining questions is optional but may still provide a learning opportunity.) Continue repeating steps three through seven until the team learns the root cause. In certain situations, the team may arrive at the point where there are no further questions to answer, but the problem remains unresolved. In these situations, it may be necessary to chart a new path to generate more questions and improve the chances of finding the root cause. Consider broadening the scope to include other potentially impacted functions or processes. Perhaps a related problem was previously not identified. The new problem may ultimately shed light on the original problem. You may also want to include a SME with fresh eyes to review the work up to this point for the following potential benefits:

- Their fresh perspective will generate questions that did not previously arise.

- They will increase the chances of introducing a previously unexploited coincidence of knowledge where an unrelated prior experience helps to connect the dots for the current situation.

Failure to formally train employees on a problem-solving framework such as the seven steps is the main reason why companies are regularly wasting corporate assets, including money and time, and negatively impacting morale with repeated problems. Failure to hold employees accountable for efficient problem-solving also lays the groundwork for an unhealthy corporate culture. Disgruntled employees with significant knowledge and expertise leave their jobs daily due to a prevailing culture of blame. Operations employees introduce inefficiencies every day by implementing workarounds rather than executing disciplined problem-solving to resolve issues permanently. These are only a couple of reasons why the vast majority of corporations are bleeding out and risking a slow, preventable death.

Below are four inefficient practices demonstrated in both professional and personal situations:

1. Avoidance via Workaround:	Implementing an inefficient or risky workaround
2. Stuck on a Theory:	Commitment to proving a theory is correct
3. Stuck on Blame:	Accusing one or more individuals of creating the problem
4. Stuck on the Wrong Problem:	Chasing the wrong problem statement

The examples that follow in the next four chapters demonstrate these inefficient practices and how each problem was subsequently resolved, in most cases, in under 7 minutes. Some of these bad habits may resonate with you, but don't get discouraged. It takes discipline and practice to retrain yourself, and you have only recently embarked on the process of understanding and committing to connecting the dots through disciplined problem-solving.

Chapter 3

Avoidance via Workaround

The workaround approach comes from placing too much emphasis on service restoration and not enough on the efficiency or scalability of the workaround itself. Service restoration is the priority in the operations space. All too often, no resource feels responsible for fixing the underlying problem. You can recognize the signs of this culture when you hear statements such as: "I provided the customer what they needed. It's not my job to fix everything broken around here."

In one such example, a business unit experienced customer issues with a tax document provided to specific customers via download from its website. The site included a link to a free Adobe trial, which was required in order to read the file. The process should have been a straightforward document download scenario. However, a few weeks before initiating the problem resolution session, the operations team began receiving calls from customers indicating that the free Adobe trial had expired. The system was now prompting customers to purchase Adobe. The customers were not willing to pay for an Adobe license simply to read the tax form. The service team agreed to manually print and physically mail these documents to customers to ensure service continuity. The focus, therefore, was solely on service restoration, and the new manual process was embraced and shared with the rest of the service team. But the new manual process was less efficient, more costly, and introduced a reputational risk due to customer dissatisfaction. Andrea, the organization leader, was eventually made aware of the issue. She recognized that the workaround was not acceptable, and she immediately implemented the disciplined framework.

The team included Andrea and one of the line managers, Bart, but not a tech resource. They felt that they could at least learn the cause of the problem even if they couldn't fix it themselves. Andrea reviewed the 7-step learning process with Bart and then proceeded to document the problem statement:

Problem Statement:

- Users are not willing to purchase the Adobe license that the system is prompting them to purchase.

They both agreed on the problem statement and moved on to listing the facts:

Facts:

- Customers reported that they were provided with a trial of a licensed version of Adobe.

- Customers reported that the trial period expired.

- This problem started three weeks ago.

- Agents implemented a workaround to print and manually mail the documents.

The team reviewed and agreed to the facts and then listed questions as follows:

Questions:

- Does the site refer them to a trial version, or is this a user error that may require clarification?

- Does the tax form need a particular version of Adobe to be read, or will the free Adobe reader suffice?

- Is this specific to a given browser or version?

- Is this specific to a unique type of customer or account?

They agreed to stop at this point, process these questions, and then assess further questions once the original questions were answered and resolved with documented facts. As the team leader, you will make the judgment call regarding whether or not to iterate through the process or wait until all questions are listed. In cases where the issue is time-sensitive or health and safety are involved, you should complete documenting as many questions as possible before assigning them for research. Since this situation was not time-critical, they agreed to iterate through the learning process. They were able to answer the first two questions quickly:

New Facts:

- Yes, the website was linking customers to a trial of a licensed version of Adobe instead of the free version of Adobe Reader.

- No, the form did not require anything more advanced than the simple, free version of Adobe Reader.

With these new facts in hand, they were able to restate the problem statement as follows:

New Problem Statement:

- The website incorrectly links customers to the paid version of Adobe instead of the free Adobe Reader.

With the root cause now clear, Bart opened a problem ticket to the technology team. The technology team implemented a simple fix with the correct link that evening. Service was restored with complete efficiency, reduced risk, and restored customer satisfaction levels by the following day. The session lasted less than 7 minutes.

Workarounds are not exclusive to the professional domain and introduce similar inefficiencies when implemented in the personal domain. For example, a home with dual-zone heating, one for upstairs and one for downstairs, was experiencing a confounding HVAC issue. Dave, the homeowner, explained that the upstairs thermostat always seemed to work fine, but the downstairs was always too cold or too hot. After numerous experiments, Dave implemented a workaround that was less than perfect but corrected the issue downstairs. Since Dave and his family were downstairs during the day, he turned off the thermostat upstairs. That workaround addressed the problem downstairs but introduced inefficiency and dissatisfaction. The upstairs would be either too hot in the summer or too cold in the winter at bedtime. This workaround, like all workarounds, only shifted the unsatisfactory experience.

As dictated by Step 1, Dave established the team to learn the root cause. The team included Dave and the local builder, Steve, who was equally intrigued by the problem. They both agreed to the accuracy of the problem statement:

Problem Statement:

- The HVAC only works correctly downstairs when the upstairs system is off.

Dave then proceeded to document the facts:

Facts:

- When the upstairs heat is on, the upstairs works fine, but the downstairs is cold.

- When the upstairs AC is on, the upstairs works fine, but the downstairs is hot.

- When the upstairs thermostat is turned off, the downstairs AC and heat both work fine.

- Each thermostat works off separate furnaces and AC units.

- The downstairs thermostat is located in the dining room on an interior wall.

- The upstairs thermostat is located in the master bedroom on an interior wall.

- A visual inspection of all components showed no apparent problems.

Dave and Steve agreed to the correctness of the facts. The next step was to document the questions.

Questions:

- Does the sun shine on the thermostat in the dining room at any point? Sun shining directly on the thermostat could heat the thermostat and cause a false reading of the room temperature.

- The thermostat is located on the wall adjoining the kitchen. Is it possible the refrigerator is heating the wall, causing a false reading of the room temperature?

- Is there any difference in the actual temperature of the wall housing the thermostat and other internal walls in the dining room?

Dave and Steve agreed that they could not think of any further questions, so they answered each of the questions as follows.

New Facts:

- The sun does not shine directly on the thermostat or the thermostat wall.

- The kitchen pantry is on the other side of the wall adjoining the thermostat, and there is nothing in the pantry generating temperature changes.

- There was a very discernable temperature difference between the wall with the thermostat and all other internal walls in the dining room.

The answer to the third question allowed Dave and Steve to restate the problem statement as:

New Problem Statement:

Something is causing temperature changes in the wall housing the downstairs thermostat, which causes false temperature readings for that thermostat.

Dave and Steve agreed that the new problem statement raised one further, and critical, question:

New Question:

- What is inside the wall that houses the downstairs thermostat?

Answering this question resulted in learning the following new facts:

New Facts:

- The ductwork for the upstairs runs from the basement to the master bedroom.

- The ductwork for the upstairs passes through the dining room wall behind the downstairs thermostat.

- The ductwork is not insulated since the wall is interior.

Dave and Steve determined the root cause for the problem in less than 7 minutes. Energy loss from the uninsulated ductwork was cooling the dining room wall in the summer and heating it in the winter. The cooling of the wall resulted in incorrect temperature readings from the thermostat downstairs. There were a few options to resolve this problem. Steve could:

1. Open the wall and insulate the ductwork.

2. Relocate the thermostat.

3. Replace the thermostat with a thermostat that utilized a remote temperature sensor to correctly gauge the temperature of whichever room Dave's family was occupying downstairs.

Dave opted for the third solution, which was successful.

Conclusion

Implementing workarounds is easily the most common approach to dealing with problems.

In her April 2018 *Educause Review* article, "Are Workarounds an Excuse to Accept Bad Process Design?" Kristine Maphis wrote:

> Our University Process Innovation (UPI) team at the University of Maryland, College Park, has done countless process assessments, and almost every process we have examined have had one thing in common: *workarounds*. Despite extremely different subjects, breadths, and complexities, each project's existing processes were littered with these supposedly temporary solutions…workplace workarounds are often shortsighted, quick fixes for identified issues in existing processes. If the workaround is uncomplicated and facilitates task completion, it may become the new way of doing business. This can lead to significant losses in productivity and missed opportunities to improve data, information, and workload as the real problem is diminished (and sometimes neglected altogether).

People implement workarounds in certain situations where service restoration or mitigation of critical health issues deprioritize problem resolution. Someone must still be responsible for ultimately connecting the dots to resolve the underlying problem. Failure to resolve the underlying problem permanently reduces the process efficiency and permanently increases the risk of future issues. No one ever built a thriving corporation on a strategy of decreasing efficiency and increasing risk.

Chapter 4

Stuck on a Theory

Individuals become stuck on a theory when they believe they know what's causing a problem, but they cannot prove it. The individual often feels that they made a mistake or will eventually find the missing information. They are hopelessly committed to figuring out what they did wrong. This behavior is pervasive with highly skilled technologists and is sometimes confused with arrogance. You can recognize this situation by statements such as, "I know what's wrong, but I just can't figure out where the mistake is." In other words, they don't know what's wrong. Technologists can get caught in this trap and only come up for air after hours, if not days, are lost.

In one such situation, a senior software developer, Chan, asked for assistance from a project manager, Crystal. Crystal was an expert in the 7-step framework. Chan explained that he and another colleague, Darius, spent all weekend researching why they were corrupting data when they read it from the cache (a fast computer memory that typically stores information temporarily).

With the team of Chan, Darius, and Crystal established, they erased a whiteboard, and Crystal started to manage the process. After a quick review, they jumped to the first iteration of the problem statement definition.

Problem Statement:

- We are corrupting data when we read it from
  the cache.

They demonstrated the issue and moved to the next step, documenting the facts.

Facts:

- When the data requested is not in the cache,
  it is read from the database and presented to the
  user with no issues.

- The system then writes the data to the cache
  for a quicker response to subsequent requests.
  The data written to the cache returns an <u>indication</u>
  <u>of success</u>. (The phrase "indication of success" is
  underlined because it raised new questions that
  are listed below.)

- When the system performs subsequent read requests,
  the data retrieved from the cache is corrupt.

With the limited set of facts documented, Crystal proceeded
to list a couple of questions.

Questions:

- Is the cache consistently corrupt each time or
  only periodically?

- Does the vendor provide a tool to interrogate the cache to confirm if the "write" was indeed successful as indicated? In other words, can the statement "the data is written to cache" be considered a fact? The code written by Chan and Darius was returning corrupt data, but they had still not confirmed that *writing* the data was working. If the system writes garbage, the system will always read garbage. The problem resolution leader can accept the existence of an error message as fact; the validity of that message, however, must always be confirmed. Take nothing for granted!

New Facts:

- In minutes, Chan used a vendor tool to query the cache and confirm that the "write to the cache" was creating corrupt data despite the message indicating success. No matter how many methods Chan and Darius implemented to read the cache, it always returned corrupted data. At this point, Crystal wrote the next pass of the problem statement, facts, and questions:

New Problem Statement:

- The system is corrupting data written to the cache despite an indication of success.

New Facts:

- The system is corrupting 100 percent of data written to the cache.

New Questions:

- Are there known issues with this function, for this vendor, for any specific product versions that caused corruption in the cache?

- Is the proper syntax being utilized for the "write" function?

New Facts:

- A quick Google search for the version of the vendor tool in use presented the following "known defect" information: "In certain scenarios, if binary compression is set to 1, corruption of data can result. In these cases, it is recommended to set binary compression to 0." Chan confirmed that binary compression was set to 1. Chan then executed a quick test with binary compression set to 0. Everything worked as expected with no corruption on the "write" to the cache or the "read" from the cache.

In this scenario, Chan and Darius were, and still are, exceptionally adept software engineers. They were both simply guilty of assuming that a vendor tool was working as expected. They both believed that they must have introduced the problem. Chan was determined to prove his theory rather than relinquish his assumption and use a more disciplined problem-solving framework to discover the answer. Once they adopted Crystal's 7-step framework, the problem was solved in less than 7 minutes.

This incident reinforces one of the most important benefits of this approach; like Crystal, you do not need to be a SME in anything other than managing the learning process. You are the problem-solving leader. You are simply guiding the SMEs to enlightenment. It may be difficult for them to avoid chasing their gut instinct with undisciplined approaches or dismissing input from others. You will need to keep them focused on answering the questions that you assign to them.

Being stuck on a theory is also not exclusive to the technology domain. Doctors diagnose problems utilizing a matching process. Most doctors, however, are not trained in the steps required to learn the root cause. The lack of problem-solving expertise dramatically delays and complicates the ultimate resolution of health issues when matching of symptoms to causes is unsuccessful.

In one such situation, Ashley, a twenty-year-old woman, was experiencing skin rashes with increasing frequency. She was an active young adult with a small dog that regularly accompanied her on hikes. Ashley was also often accompanied by friends and their pets. None of the other individuals were experiencing similar issues.

Ashley visited numerous doctors who investigated the rashes on her legs, arms, and neck. Following standard diagnostic practices, each doctor explained it looked like a topical reaction to something she came in contact with while hiking.

Ashley asked how the reaction could occur on her neck, arms, and legs if she had not strayed from the hiking trail. The doctors indicated that the allergen might transfer to her from her dog. Some suggested that Ashley undergo allergy testing. While it is always good to obtain more facts, unfortunately, the only facts obtained from the testing were that Ashley was not allergic to any tested allergens. To gather additional facts, some doctors asked if Ashley had changed detergents or shampoos recently; she had not. Ashley's doctors then concluded that external environmental exposure caused the reaction. They offered suggestions to protect herself, such as making sure her skin was covered while hiking. They also prescribed various skin creams to address the symptoms of the reaction.

Fortunately, Ashley was no stranger to the importance of using the 7-step framework to empower her own health-care advocacy. Ashley collaborated with her hiking partner, Eleanor, to see if they could solve the problem themselves. As they iterated through the process, they could add medical experts if required. But for now, they started with the problem statement.

Problem Statement:

- Rashes randomly appear on Ashley's arms, legs, and neck.

Once they were in agreement on the problem statement, they moved on to list the facts and questions.

Facts:

- The rashes all appear to be similar, at least visually.

- The rashes only started in the last year.

- The rashes are increasing in frequency and severity.

- The rashes can happen any day, not just the days she hikes.

- The rashes can occur any time of day, although they usually start in the late morning.

- They are not aware of any significant environmental change coinciding with the rash's appearance, such as detergent, clothing material, shampoo, living quarters, dog shampoo, etc.

- The rashes occur while traveling out of town without her dog.

They both agreed that these were the relevant facts they were aware of, so they moved on to the questions.

Questions:

- Does Ashley have any other known allergies?

- Has Ashley's stress level changed significantly in the last year?

- Have Ashley's dietary habits changed materially in the previous year?

- Does Ashley know anyone else having similar issues during the same period?

- Has Ashley experienced any other physical reactions during the same time frame?

Once they listed these questions, they circled back to answer whichever they could and seek help as necessary from other SMEs.

Facts:

- As a child, Ashley had severe reactions to antibiotic sulfa drugs (sulfonamides). This information was also previously provided to all doctors via her standard patient profile.

- Stress levels have been pretty consistent for the last couple of years.

- Dietary habits were reasonably consistent for the last couple of years.

- Ashley was not aware of any friends experiencing similar issues.

- An increase in canker sores was the only additional, notable physical change during this period. (Remember, no fact is too small or too insignificant to capture.)

These new facts led to a couple of further questions.

New Questions:

- Can sulfa allergies cause skin reactions?

- What can cause an increase in canker sores?

Ashley and Eleanor agreed that it was time to supplement the team with another SME. They added to the team a dentist, Tim, to assist with the canker sore question. After they shared with Tim the process and the new questions it had produced, he immediately remarked that one of his family members was recently diagnosed with a severe allergy to sulfates (chemicals used as cleansing agents). The sulfate in their toothpaste was causing frequent canker sores. This revelation immediately led to a series of new questions.

New Questions:

- What foods did Ashley consume that had sulfites or sulfates?

- Did Ashley's shampoo, soap, detergent, toothpaste, etc., include sulfates?

After reviewing Ashley's food and cleansers for a few minutes, they were able to determine the following new facts:

Facts:

- Virtually every cleaner used by Ashley contained sulfates or sulfites.

- Many foods in Ashley's diet included sulfites. Some sulfites occur naturally in food and beverages, such as red wines.

All indications pointed to the root cause being an increasingly severe reaction to anything containing sulfates or sulfites. Ashley decided to remove sulfites and sulfates from her life wherever possible. Ashley scrutinized shampoos, detergents, lotions (some of which, ironically, were provided by doctors to treat the rash). The impact was an immediate and complete elimination of allergic skin reactions and a significant reduction in the occurrence of canker sores. Living with the knowledge of the actual root cause has been life-changing for

Ashley for the last two years and counting. The time invested in this exercise—less than an hour that included contacting the additional SME—was time well spent even if it was more than 7 minutes.

This story underscores the importance of including a diverse set of SMEs, walking them through the process, and listening to them. Coincidental knowledge, like Tim's information regarding sulfates, often enables the learning process. Coincidence and luck can play a significant role in solving many problems. As the problem resolution team leader, it is your responsibility to position the team to be exposed to luck or coincidence and to take advantage of it when it occurs.

Conclusion

Consistently exercising the discipline to follow this methodology will release you from the burden of proving theories. Theories are constructive only as tools to generate questions. Removing the burden of chasing pet theories will significantly make your time pursuing answers more productive and creative. In a 2019 ActiveState survey of 1,250 software developers from eighty-eight countries, responders indicated spending approximately 7.4 percent of their time investigating production bugs and security issues. Undisciplined developers spin their wheels attempting to prove pet theories when these bugs arise. Preventing these errors from entering production is a topic for another book and often involves very costly solutions. In the meantime, there is a clear opportunity to reduce the burden by introducing and reinforcing the discipline of formal problem-solving as a more effective means of connecting the dots.

Chapter 5

Stuck on Blame

Many organizations promote ineffective behaviors. A culture of blame, for example, can impact an entire organization's ability to resolve problems. An organization that fosters a culture of blame typically expends more energy trying to prove an individual or team introduced a problem rather than trying to learn what caused the problem. A culture of blame not only inhibits learning and innovation but can create an extremely toxic environment.

One common source of the blame approach is known as PEBKAC (pronounced "pehb kack"), a call center or support desk term. It can be used interchangeably as a noun or adjective, as in, "I think this is a PEBKAC," or, "This is a PEBKAC problem." It stands for "Problem Exists Between Keyboard And Chair," a wry way of saying the person in the chair is the problem. There is no question that many service desk interactions are user errors, and in these cases, a skilled agent will shift into a respectful training mode to train the user on the proper usage. However, operations team members often apply the user error label when the underlying problem is not so easily proven or reproduced. In some cases, the problem makes no sense to the SMEs based on their understanding of how the technology works. You will recognize this situation when you hear statements like, "Well, we know what we implemented works for everyone else, so the user must be doing something wrong."

Incidents of blame often spike with the introduction of new technology and processes. The introduction of VoIP (Voice over Internet Protocol), for example, was a significant change for all companies. Amy, a service desk manager at a major retail financial institution, was responsible for servicing customers during the transition to VoIP. The implementation team identified and resolved all of the initial problems they encountered. Once the dust settled, however, there were persistent reports of issues in certain branches. The initial consensus was that the users were doing something to cause the problem, since it was limited to those branches. The general health of the system was checked and appeared to be okay. Problem tickets were investigated and closed with the comment, "Problem no longer exists and could not be reproduced."

But the branch managers continued to report this issue as premium customers kept complaining that phone calls were disconnected at about the same time agents' computers rebooted. The customers were not pleased with this recurring issue and threatened to take their business elsewhere. The leadership team responsible for the upgrade had to establish a task force to research the problem. As a member of this task force and an expert in the 7-step framework, Amy took the initiative to visit a couple of impacted branches. Her goal was to gather facts in person to share with the task force. She witnessed the situation and confirmed that the agents were doing their jobs as instructed and yet the system was not performing as expected. Following her visit, Amy provided the task force with the following:

Problem Statement:

- Phone calls are dropping mid-conversation, causing agents to wait for the PC to reboot before using the phone again.

Facts:

- The phone calls were dropping mid-conversation.

- The PCs rebooted at roughly the same time calls were dropped.

- The PCs rebooted whether or not they were in active use.

- The reboots occurred only in specific branches.

- The reboots occurred with multiple employees in the impacted branches.

Questions:

- What was required for VoIP to work? In other words, what was the flow of data into the branch and to the agent's phone?

- Was there a difference between these components in branches that had issues and those that did not? In other words, did each branch use the same technology? With the same capacity? On the same computers?

Amy shared these facts and questions with the task force and requested that they provide the answers as soon as possible. After getting responses, she then recorded the following new facts:

New Facts:

- The technology used to provide internet data to the branches was not the same for all branches. In particular, the impacted branches were all running with a significantly lower bandwidth for internet data than the unaffected branches.

- The addition of voice data to the digital channel pushed the bandwidth beyond the stated capacity.

- The resulting bandwidth issues were causing the PC to reboot. The VoIP data flows through the PC to the phone. When the PC rebooted, the calls were lost.

These new facts led to a modification of the problem statement accordingly:

New Problem Statement:

- Insufficient internet bandwidth was causing PC and phone issues in certain branches.

This scenario required more than 7 minutes, because Amy did not have access to the required SMEs during the branch fact gathering, demonstrating that timely access to SMEs is critical. Although Amy was fortunate that the SMEs on the task force could resolve this issue fairly quickly once they were contacted, the delay in focusing on formal problem-solving had an impact on the firm's reputation. Erosion of reputation is yet another way that corporations can slowly bleed to death.

Uncertainty exists when no one is explicitly responsible for resolving a problem. This gray area often leads to finger-pointing among interested parties. Unanswered questions will lead to blame and heightened emotions due to the lack of focus on connecting the dots using disciplined problem-solving.

This is true with personal as well as professional situations. In another example, an educator informed Debbie and Mark that their young daughter, Kelsey, was not "living up to expectations." The educator proposed several theories, including laziness, lack of focus, and a limited desire to participate. Mark and Debbie were both hard-working and well-educated and assumed their daughter was the same, so this feedback came as a surprise to them. Mark and Debbie initially responded by providing support to Kelsey with a mix of rewards for jobs well-done and appropriate punishment for work not performed. After a few months in this state of escalated attention, the parents privately shared that they were not seeing laziness, lack of focus, or a lack of desire to participate. However, they saw a level of frustration from Kelsey that neither experienced when they had been students. Kelsey found simple exercises tedious and time-consuming. Kelsey found challenging assignments to be almost impossible, often resulting in emotional outbursts of frustration. At one point, Kelsey spent hours trying to read a single sentence from an easy book, but she was unable to get past reading "as" as two separate letters: "A…S." Ultimately, she broke down in tears. As opposed to the educator's theories, there was never a lack of focus or an unwillingness to work.

Debbie and Mark shared these observations at a subsequent parent-teacher meeting. They were hoping to hear new ideas from an educator regarding what they should try next. The educator indicated that the school tested Kelsey over the last few years and found no indications of learning or processing disorders. Hence, they were unsure what else to try. Debbie and Mark began to suspect that the educator did not have the desire or training to investigate Kelsey's particular circumstances, resorting to unfair characterizations of their daughter's disposition. Beyond teaching the curriculum and making Debbie and Mark aware of any lack of effort or apparent issues with Kelsey, the teachers believed they were not responsible for resolving any underlying problems.

Debbie and Mark then consulted with a pediatrician who confirmed that Kelsey was in perfect physical health. Debbie and Mark were disappointed in Kelsey for not being able to do the schoolwork and disappointed in themselves for not being able to help her succeed. Meanwhile, the teachers were blaming Kelsey, while Debbie and Mark were blaming the teachers.

All of this added up to a stalemate. Whether at home or in the workplace, a culture of blame often leads to an unproductive impasse. A stalemate should signal that you are in a blame situation, and it is time to be disciplined about implementing a problem-solving framework.

Fortunately for Debbie and Mark, they were both trained in this framework and recognized that it was time to use it to support their advocacy needs. As indicated by the process, the first step was to build the team. For this situation, the team included Debbie, Mark, and Kelsey's teacher. Educating the teacher on the process, Step 2, helped diminish emotional bias and finger-pointing. They could then proceed to the problem statement step.

Problem Statement:

- Learning, for Kelsey, appears to be much more complicated than it should be, even when the material is well below grade level.

Facts were then listed as follows:

Facts:

- Math, reading, and science are extremely challenging for Kelsey on her own.

- When discussed verbally, Kelsey can understand most things well.

- Kelsey is not distracted in class, and her behavior is solid.

- Kelsey appears to be very determined to learn, although often stressed about the difficulties.

- Kelsey's art projects are all excellent and demonstrate a significant effort on her part.

- Kelsey is willing to work on homework jointly with her parents but can often get frustrated.

- Kelsey does not appear to present any physiological issues.

- All tests performed by the school indicate that no problem exists that could be detected by those tests.

Many questions followed. Some of the key questions are listed below:

Questions:

- At what grade level is Kelsey able to demonstrate mastery in each subject compared to her actual grade level?

- How has Kelsey performed on eye tests and hearing tests?

- Are there more extensive tests to perform?

- Are other kids in the class struggling similarly?

- Where does Kelsey physically sit in the class?

Mark and Debbie documented the answers to these questions as follows:

New Facts:

- Kelsey was reading well below her seventh-grade level.

- Kelsey passed all recent eye and hearing tests.

- Yes, additional tests existed, but the school was not willing to pay for them. Educators never performed formal disability testing.

- The class is a typical seventh-grade class from the perspective of participation and behavior.

- Kelsey physically sits in the middle of the class.

Mark and Debbie realized that they must add a new subject matter expert to the team. In particular, they required an educational psychologist specializing in developmental learning and processing. Since neither the school nor insurance viewed this as their responsibility, Debbie and Mark were left to identify, schedule, and pay for the proper testing themselves. Testing was performed and confirmed that Kelsey was reading at a kindergarten level and suffered from extreme dyslexia.

The teacher reviewed and accepted the new test results as facts. All parties agreed to the root cause:

Root Cause:

- Kelsey has severe dyslexia and requires widely proven and accepted accommodations to enable her learning.

It is important to note that there were also many ancillary questions, including how a child with such a gap in reading ability made it as far as Kelsey did. When trying to solve a challenging problem, you must remain focused on the problem statement. The problem resolution leader should record tangential questions about broken monitoring steps that failed to identify symptoms of the issue. However, the problem resolution leader should also defer discussing these questions until after the root cause is determined, since they can be distracting and may reignite finger-pointing. Managing emotions during the learning process is a critical responsibility of the problem-solving leader.

Dyslexia, unfortunately, is one such problem that falls into the gray area of responsibility and accountability in the educational system. Personal problems that fall into gray areas call for personal advocacy. Parents of people with dyslexia are often required to advocate strongly for their children. As noted in the University of Michigan's "Dyslexia Myths and Facts":

> Dyslexia is not characterized as a medical problem and is not typically diagnosed by doctors because they don't have training in oral language, reading, writing, or spelling assessment and diagnosis. That said, developmental pediatricians have additional training in cognition and learning, and some have expertise in the clinical and neurobiological features of dyslexia. There is no pill or medication that can heal dyslexia. Additionally, dyslexia is typically not covered by medical insurance (i.e., it is not a medical problem), although it does have lifelong negative effects that can encompass feelings of wellbeing.

In Kelsey's situation, the school department implemented proper accommodations for her. Thanks to these accommodations and her own determination, drive, and intelligence, she is now a successful software engineer.

Conclusion

In *The Oxford Review*, Adrienne Hardwick writes that a culture of blame leads to:

- Higher levels of turnover

- Reduced work engagement and productivity

- Decision escalation, or continually referring to managers for decisions

- Lower levels of organizational performance

- Lower levels of innovation behaviors and creativity

- Reduced levels of job satisfaction

- Reduced levels of responsibility taking

Contrast this with the following observation from "Building a Problem-Solving Culture That Lasts," written by Randy Cook and Alison Jenkins from the McKinsey consulting firm:

Building a problem-solving culture that lasts is not about fixing particular problems but about always striving to do things better. Eliminating long-standing niggles and introducing more efficient ways of working are not the only gains; companies with a well-established problem-solving culture also benefit from the strength of the capabilities people develop and the engagement and enthusiasm they bring to their work. These give organizations the means and the momentum to sustain their performance in the future.

If your organization is experiencing some of the characteristics Hardwick lists, it is time to consider supporting empowered, disciplined problem-solving and eliminating blame. Leaders in problem-solving reward their teams for pulling together a diverse team to connect the dots and fix problems in a disciplined manner. Leaders in problem-solving do not reward teams for blaming or accusing others. The change may not be immediate—cultural change is difficult overall—but reducing negativity across partnering teams will help precipitate cultural change as well as joint productivity over time.

Chapter 6

Stuck on the Wrong Problem

Continuing to ask the wrong question will always get you an answer you don't need. You will waste time and exhaust yourself looking for a penny in the corner of a round room. As we have seen in the previous examples, restating the original problem is more the norm than the exception. For this reason, the 7-step framework explicitly prescribes that the problem leader revisit the problem statement as the process iterates.

After arriving at the office at 7:30 a.m., Josh, a technology operations manager, greeted Gaurav, a resource from the operations team. Gaurav asked if Josh could assist with an issue that occurred during the nightly processing. The team was aware that Josh was very experienced in leading the 7-step learning process. Gaurav presented the initial problem statement as, "The process said it ran successfully but it didn't do any of the updates it was supposed to do." Gaurav continued with the proposed root cause: "The database team must have changed something to cause this problem, but that team isn't in yet, so we can't prove it." The culture of blame within this particular team was quite pervasive. Josh immediately grabbed a whiteboard and went to work. Since it was still early and the database team remained unavailable, Josh created the initial team with Gaurav and Shane, a software engineer. Josh knew that he could add other SMEs if required later. First, Josh revisited the problem statement and adjusted it slightly from Gaurav's original wording as follows:

Problem Statement:

- The process did not perform any of the expected updates when it ran this morning.

Josh confirmed that the team agreed with this statement and then documented the facts and a few questions as follows:

Facts:

- The process returned a code indicating successful completion.

- The process run time was fractions of a second, which was much faster than usual.

- The process did not perform any updates.

- There were easily verified instances of updates that should have occurred.

Questions:

- What criteria must be met for the updates to occur?

  » Data?

  » Various constraints?

  » Other process predecessors?

  » General logic built into the code?

- Did the process run successfully yesterday? Were there any errors?

Josh asked Shane to chase down any errors from yesterday's cycle Josh reviewed the code to document any conditions controlling the execution of the process. It was only a matter of minutes before Josh could list new facts and cycle back to Step 3.

New Facts:

- The process ran successfully yesterday with no errors, and updates were processed.

- Before execution, the process checks a control flag to ensure that the process did not already run on that calendar date. Previously, this process ran twice on the same day, so the operations team implemented the control flag to ensure that it would never happen again. (Notice that the control flag is a workaround instead of a solution to the duplicate execution. We've already discussed the costs and risks of workarounds. Introducing this workaround planted the seeds of future issues, which would only grow over time.)

Josh revisited the problem statement based on the new facts but did not have sufficient information to change it, so it remained unchanged. He referenced the new facts to ask an additional question.

New Question:

- What was the value of the control flag when the unsuccessful process started?

New Fact:

- The control flag incorrectly indicated the process already ran for that calendar date. The incorrect state of the flag forced the process to run without performing any updates.

At this point, Josh restated the original problem statement correctly.

New Problem Statement:

- The process control flag was not in the correct state to enable proper process execution.

The root cause of the problem was determined to be the failure of a process that resets the flag. This failure was not monitored and, therefore, not detected. The process that failed to perform updates ran because it was not dependent on the successful execution of the flag reset process. That night, the operations team implemented a simple check for the successful completion of that process. In conjunction with the right SMEs, Josh used this framework to resolve the problem in under 7 minutes rather than wasting hours waiting for another team to arrive.

As you can probably imagine, being stuck on the wrong problem is not exclusive to the professional realm. For example, as a parent, the challenge of dealing with a child who starts to demonstrate a propensity for bending the truth is as tough as any problem you will solve in your professional career.

In one particular case, a teenager, Sarah, demonstrated early signs of heading down the path of deception with her parents, Sue and Paul. When communicating plans for the upcoming weekend, Sarah's information progressively deviated from the truth. Sue and Paul assessed the situation and initially landed on the same problem statement: "It's that new kid Sarah is hanging out with!" Granted, this is another scenario where a culture of blame rather than disciplined problem-solving can lose time and potentially imperil relationships; it can also lead to an incorrect problem statement. Sue and Paul did not want to go to the extreme of forbidding the new friend, so they opted for more moderate privilege removal. Weeks passed with further deterioration of the relationship and no end to Sarah's deceptions. The punishments provided no relief from the lying and only served to further fracture their relationship with Sarah.

Sue and Paul realized that the methods that worked when Sarah was five years old were no longer working with their teenager; a new approach was required. Sue and Paul decided to try formal problem-solving since they felt like they had no other options and they were both familiar with the 7-step framework. They proceeded to Step 1, which was to build the team. The team would naturally include Sue, Paul, and Sarah. They realized that other experts could potentially be required later, but no one was more expert in the current situation than they were.

As the process dictates, the next step was to train the team on the approach and gain agreement before proceeding. With the team pulled together in the kitchen, Sue and Paul walked

Sarah through the process. To entice full participation, Sue offered to remove all privilege restrictions with the successful completion of the exercise. This offer was met by Sarah with a skeptical willingness to participate. With the tension temporarily relieved, Sue and Paul moved to Step 3. All parties agreed to the following problem statement:

Problem Statement:

- Numerous lies were told recently.

The easy part was complete. It was time to dive headfirst into the facts, which were essentially a list of Sarah's lies over the past few weeks. This list will likely be familiar to parents as well as any of us who were typical teenagers.

Facts:

- There were lies about the destination for the evening.

- There were lies about who or how many people would be there.

- There were lies about whether or not parents would be home.

- There were lies about who was driving.

- There were lies about whether or not people would be consuming alcohol.

Note that the problem statement and facts, as written, are in the passive voice, focusing on the content of the lies instead of who said them. Avoiding the culture of blame is difficult, but it's a critical factor in the success of this scenario. As much as Sarah had no interest in rehashing what was discussed ad nauseam over the last few weeks, the promise of having her restrictions ended encouraged her to agree that these fact statements were accurate. These statements led to the following question, asked by Sue:

Question:

- Why were these lies communicated?

After pondering the question for a few minutes, Sarah decided that this was her opportunity to head full steam down the path of honesty while also having all restrictions removed. She responded with a new set of precise, albeit emotionally conveyed, facts.

New Facts:

- I lied because you don't trust me.

- If I tell you I'm going to a party, you won't let me go.

- If I tell you the parents won't be home, you won't let me go.

- If I tell you kids will be drinking alcohol, you won't let me go.

Sarah then finished with the statement, "I think we can all agree those are facts!!" Sue and Paul nervously grinned and nodded in affirmation. The respect offered by this collective affirmation is an excellent example of the importance of confirming every team member's agreement on the new facts. Before proceeding, Sue proposed that the problem statement should be updated as follows:

New Problem Statement:

- There was a severe lack of trust in both directions between Sue and Paul and Sarah.

With a bit of hesitation and a few comments along the lines of feeling like this was a therapy session, all agreed to accept the new problem statement. They proceeded to document the next set of questions.

New Questions:

- How do we build a foundation of trust?

- Why do you think we don't want you at parties that can get out of control?

- Why do you think we don't want you driven by someone who drank alcohol?

Everyone started to let their guard down as emotions remained in check and arms were unfolding. After a few moments, Paul provided some encouragement that this was progressing well. This discussion was their most productive one in months.

Sarah, after some hesitation, agreed to provide the answers to the most recent questions.

New Facts:

- Paul and Sue care about Sarah's future and safety.

- The school will suspend all students caught at parties where alcohol is involved; Sue and Paul do not want Sarah suspended.

- Sue and Paul care about the property of other families and don't want Sarah present if destructive behavior is occurring.

Paul and Sue mentioned all of these facts during previous heated arguments. Unfortunately, facts presented in the heat of the moment, in an unstructured manner, are often not received as intended. The emotional ineffectiveness of unstructured communication is also a factor in professional settings.

With agreement on the new facts and the final problem statement, Sue and Paul proposed a solution. Paul, Sue, and Sarah negotiated a list of criteria to serve as the basis for building a foundation of trust in the future. They agreed on this and set out to create the list, which included the following items:

- If no parents were home and more than ten kids arrived, it would be time to leave. (Sue and Paul wanted eight, and Sarah wanted fifteen; ten was the compromise.)

- If people were noticeably drunk, it would be time to leave.

- Only someone who was not drinking would drive Sarah home. If that option did not exist, Sarah would call Sue and Paul for a ride, and there would be no punishment, since Sarah made a good decision.

- If boys start fighting, it will be time to leave.

- If people are not respecting the property, it is time to leave.

- If the plans change, Sue and Paul will be notified immediately, at least via text.

All parties agreed to these terms. Sue and Paul lifted all active restrictions. As the first Friday evening arrived, Sarah had a noticeable bounce in her step. There was a lot of nervous anticipation of this first evening out under the new pact of honesty. During dinner, Sue asked Sarah what she was doing that night. "Going to Kristen's house to hang out" was her response. Sue asked if Kristen's parents would be home, to which Sarah gleefully answered "nope." Sue then asked how many kids would be there, to which Sarah responded, "about six that I know of." Paul then calmly reinforced the criteria of the trust agreement. Dinner continued peacefully, and shortly after that, Sarah left for the evening's activities. At approximately 11:00 p.m., Sue and Paul received a call from Sarah. Sarah was now outside of a fast-food restaurant where she drove with a few friends. She explained that too many people showed up, kids were getting drunk, and the inevitable scene of boys fighting on the front lawn had developed quickly. Sarah recognized that numerous boxes were checked, grabbed her friends, jumped in her car, and drove away. As they drove down the street, they passed two police cars quickly heading in the opposite direction. The police went to Kristen's home and collected the names of all who were still in the house. Because there were underage students at the party consuming alcohol, all attendees were suspended from school the following week. Meanwhile, Sarah had followed the criteria and her parents had lived up to their promises; trust was earned that night in both directions. In this case, admitting that trust issues existed and developing a plan to address the problem became another example of a 7-minute session that changed lives forever.

Conclusion

You've likely heard the famous quote attributed to Albert Einstein regarding the importance of the correct problem statement:

If I were given one hour to save the planet,
I would spend fifty-nine minutes defining the problem
and one minute resolving it.

Failure to recognize that you have the wrong problem statement will delay, if not wholly prevent, the inevitable learning required for the root cause to be understood and the right dots to be connected. Facts, rather than theories and accusations, will eventually lead to the correct problem statement. As the problem-solving leader, it is your responsibility to ensure that the learning process continues to move forward in the right direction. Taking the time to revisit and confirm agreement on the new problem statement will ensure forward progress. Actively replacing the old problem statement with the new one will prevent the wasteful trap of endlessly revisiting a false premise.

Chapter 7

Stop the Bleeding

As you've seen in the previous examples, it is common to observe at least two of the four undisciplined behaviors when dealing with challenging problems. In this final, extremely personal story, you will see all of the behaviors discussed previously. The behaviors were exhibited by the best and brightest in the medical profession from New York to Boston. This example is particularly personal as it deals with the thirteen-year challenge of solving my wife's very rare bleeding disorder. During this journey, I witnessed these experts implementing ineffective, if not dangerous, workarounds, being stuck on theories or incorrect problem statements, and ultimately resorting to blame. All of these behaviors were just as ineffective in solving her rare bleeding disorder as any other business or personal problem.

In 1989, Kim, my twenty-five-year-old wife of three years, held out her upper left arm, winced in pain, and commented that her arm hurt. At that moment, having no formal training in disciplined problem-solving, I ran through my limited repertoire of responses. I started by making her an ice pack for the bruise, but it hurt so bad she could not hold ice on the affected area. I then suggested that she take an anti-inflammatory, go to sleep, and check it again in the morning. Unfortunately, the pain was so intense that she was not able to sleep. My father proposed our third option: he suggested that we go to a teaching hospital, like Columbia Presbyterian in Manhattan, due to the apparent unique nature of the situation. Kim agreed, so we made our way there.

At the hospital, there was a refreshing sense of curiosity and eagerness among the staff to identify the root cause. With that said, the night dragged on without answers or much relief for Kim's pain. There was also a distinct lack of urgency from doctors and nurses since this did not appear to be life-threatening. A continuous parade of doctors, students, specialists, and nurses all stopped by to take their shot at matching the known symptoms to known causes. There were many interesting, albeit random, insights but no root cause or singular sense of responsibility for resolving the issue.

Eventually, there was increased concern regarding what appeared to be continued internal bleeding. One doctor had the foresight to use a ballpoint pen to circle the bruise to track expansion. In a matter of hours, the bruise was spreading down her upper arm and also changing colors, from purple to orange to yellow; this was nothing Kim had ever experienced before. She and I had the distinct sense that none of the doctors had ever seen this before. By the following day, doctors noted that her fingers had swelled to the size of sausages. Kim's wrist was so swollen that her mobility was limited, and the pain was excruciating. This moment was the first time in my life that I experienced a sense of abject failure due to my inability to solve a severe problem impacting someone I loved. I did not yet have the tools or discipline required to solve this very challenging problem. I was in no way prepared to serve as a problem-solving leader or advocate for the care of someone I loved. Feeling helpless, I deferred to the experts, as so many people do every day.

It was becoming clear that Kim's doctors diagnosed health concerns by matching known symptoms to known causes. They did not utilize formal problem-solving to *learn* the cause of health issues, and they often filled the problem-solving void with misguided and ineffective behaviors.

Over the next few days—yes, *days*—at Columbia Presbyterian, numerous tests were conducted and then conducted again. Doctors tested Kim for factor-XIII-related disorders such as hemophilia. They were all false. Despite the false tests and no prior history of clotting issues, the doctors still theorized that Kim had a factor XIII problem. The doctors doubled down and reran the tests. Einstein is also credited with saying, "Doing the same thing over and over while expecting different results is the definition of insanity." We were officially stuck on a theory.

Eventually, tests were also performed for soft tissue disorders; they came out false. Tests were performed for autoimmune diseases; they came out false. Everything was false. Instead of focusing on what we knew about the facts associated with Kim's situation, the doctors were tragically heading down a path of disproving various theories of what it could be. Many of these theories had no connection to the facts we openly shared with every doctor who inquired. When theories proved to be fruitless and frustrating for the doctors and us, we then witnessed the transition into workaround behavior.

It no longer made sense to use a pen to circle the swelling on Kim's arm unless you circled her arm at her armpit with an arrow pointing down. The doctors realized that they had to treat the symptoms more aggressively. Kim was at risk of compartment syndrome, a significant increase in internal pressure that can damage nerves and muscles. The treatment selected was to use an aggressive dose of the steroid prednisone.

The prednisone treatment worked as the swelling eventually subsided and the pain slowly diminished. Kim was released from the hospital a few days and tens of thousands of insurance dollars later. She remained on a maintenance dosage of prednisone for months. The doctor slowly decreased the prednisone dose, and Kim resumed her everyday life. As she tapered off the medication, we all held our collective breath and prayed that the bleeding did not return. Thankfully, it did not. Prescribing prednisone, although a workaround, was the correct step to take given the situation's urgency. But as is typical with the "workaround" approach, no one remained focused on resolving the actual problem following its implementation. In the years that followed, Kim gave birth to our two daughters. Both were full-term, relatively small babies, and both were very healthy. Within the next few years, there were no additional bleeding episodes.

Our third child was due on September 26, 1994, seven months after we relocated to Boston. By all accounts, things were progressing normally. We were only one day from Kim's due date when she woke me in the morning with a look of grave concern. She indicated that it was too long since she had felt the baby kick, and she was very concerned. Without hesitation, we made our way to the hospital. An examination confirmed that we had lost our child one day before Kim's due date. One of the worst of life's most challenging problems was our new reality.

One day later, we returned to the hospital for the stillbirth of our only son, Cody. We were very fortunate to have the support of a nurse, Peggy, at the hospital who coached us through what was about to happen. Most importantly, she convinced us to spend time with our son and also to have an autopsy. There is nothing I could ever say or do to thank Peggy for being there for us on that day. The importance of gathering facts was certainly not at the forefront of my thought process on the most emotional day of my life. Fortunately, we both listened to her advice and followed her suggestions.

In the months that followed, we started to ask critical questions: How could this happen? Are we able to have more children? The results of the autopsy only raised more questions. Cody's placenta had been 40 percent infarcted, or calcified, on Kim's expected due date. The placenta should not be that infarcted until many weeks after the due date. With 40 percent calcification, Cody simply was not receiving the nutrition required to sustain life. We still had no answers regarding why the placenta was in that state on Kim's due date.

Kim was now living with two significant medical mysteries at the young age of thirty: What caused the bleeding problem in 1989, and why was our son's placenta 40 percent calcified on her due date in 1994?

As discussed in the dyslexia case, the gray area of responsibility is always a warning sign that you must assume the role of advocate yourself. If no one else views your problem as cleanly falling into their primary area of expertise, no one will feel a vested interest in solving the problem. Kim's medical condition was solidly in that gray area. She recognized the situation and assumed the role of advocate for her care. She maintained immaculate records with dates of each event, treatments, comments, theories, and observations. Kim's records would prove to be a critical source of facts we would eventually use in the 7-step framework. When dealing with unresolved recurring problems, every occurrence of a problem is an opportunity to gather more facts. Even if the facts are simply the date, time, and weather, you can never have too many facts, but you can most certainly have too few. All facts are additional pieces to the very daunting jigsaw puzzle that lies before you.

In 1997, during a ski trip, Kim took a fall on the slopes that caused a tear in her ACL. Upon returning home, she required arthroscopic surgery. The surgery went as expected, and Kim eventually transitioned into physical therapy for her knee. Approximately three months after surgery, while at physical therapy, Kim showed signs of what evolved into her second episode of massive internal hemorrhaging. The doctors in Massachusetts were quick to tell us that they wanted to rush Kim into surgery to rule out potentially fatal necrotizing fasciitis (NF, also known as flesh-eating disease). Although we both knew that this was not NF, they assured us that the surgery would only require one-inch incisions on each side of her lower calf. We agreed to this procedure based on their assurances and mentioned that we looked forward to discussing the prednisone dose once the procedure was complete.

As a side note, you must always remain calm when dealing with challenging operational problems or medical advocacy situations. It was certainly frustrating to hear the doctors dismiss our insistence that Kim required prednisone, but even these moments are important opportunities to gather facts. It remained the right thing to do if the incisions were relatively harmless and could lead to new discoveries, such as the origin of bleeding.

After waiting for what seemed like hours, the lead surgeon emerged and confirmed that she did not have NF. They did not, however, learn anything new about the source of bleeding. Unfortunately, this meant that we were now back in the same situation as when her arm experienced massive internal hemorrhaging in 1989. The doctors eventually honored our request and administered prednisone as the mitigating workaround. But once again, no one assumed responsibility for anything resembling formal problem-solving. We were still solidly in the gray area of problem resolution with no clear accountability for her medical care.

Three years passed with no bleeding episodes when, in 2000, Kim tripped on the threshold from the garage into our house and broke a bone in her hand. We were once again off to a hospital—this time in Boston—to have a pin surgically implanted into her hand. The surgeon performed the surgery with no issues; however, roughly three months later, Kim recognized the familiar dime-sized purple circle on her arm. Again, excruciating pain accompanied the new black and blue mark. A third bleeding episode was underway, and it was spreading quickly. We quickly drove to Brigham and Women's Hospital in Boston. By the time we arrived, her arm was extremely swollen and showing various colors, including the familiar purple, orange, and yellow. Her arm appeared as though she had been the victim of spousal abuse; it looked as though she had been grabbed or hit multiple times. Not surprisingly, the ER staff questioned us separately to rule out spousal abuse. This questioning process is critical and completely valid; it just wasn't the issue in our case. Once Kim received the attention of senior staff, we shared the entire history of her bleeding episodes. We mentioned that the sooner they could administer prednisone, the sooner Kim would be out of pain, and we could begin to discuss what was causing the bleeding. The doctors assured me that they would take care of Kim, but they dismissed my input. Remember, when documenting questions, you must keep an open mind and two open ears to consider all potential input. Failure to do so will delay, if not hinder, the learning process.

The doctors were, once again, concerned about compartment syndrome. They were so worried that they rushed her to surgery instead of administering prednisone. They opened her right forearm with an incision approximately six inches long and left it open to relieve the pressure. Internal inspections were not able to locate the source of bleeding, given that blood was everywhere. More than the prednisone, this surgery was an even more drastic workaround that provided no additional helpful information regarding the underlying bleeding disorder, and it left Kim with a large permanent scar on her forearm. This workaround also involved performing surgery, which increasingly looked like more of a problem than a solution.

Doctors ran a barrage of tests while Kim recovered in the hospital. The majority of these tests, once again, were for clotting disorders and factor-XIII-related issues. Other conditions were also considered, such as autoimmune issues like rheumatoid arthritis (RA), despite few, if any, typical indicators of RA. In particular, Kim demonstrated no issues with joints that would normally be associated with RA. Instead of focusing on how the bleeding process works and identifying what part of that process was not working correctly, the doctors doubled down on their efforts to match known symptoms in column A to known causes in column B. Not surprisingly, they found no clear link.

By late 2000, we were more than eleven years into the bleeding mystery and still languishing in the gray area of responsibility. Attempting to prove pet theories failed. Implementing workarounds delayed focus on the core problem and left Kim permanently disfigured and no closer to a root cause.

The difference between this third hospitalization and all prior treatments was that this visit included a surgical workaround. Three months after the third bleeding episode, Kim was once again experiencing significant pain in the arm that had been splayed open previously. She was experiencing her fourth bleeding episode only three months after the last one. We made the familiar journey to Brigham and Women's hospital to meet with the heads of hematology for both Brigham and Women's and the Dana Farber Cancer Institute. Now they decided that it was time to take the workaround step even further. They reopened Kim's arm to relieve the pressure, but instead of letting it remain open until the bleeding subsided, they took a skin graft from her hip and placed it on the wound in her arm. The theory was that this would allow her arm to swell until the bleeding stopped, expanding enough to prevent the painful symptoms of compartment syndrome. This procedure would avoid surgery in three months if it happened again and hopefully break the cycle.

Between 2000 and 2001, Kim's medical bills exceeded $1 million, and we were not even a tiny bit closer to solving the problem. We had spent a lot of insurance money, as well as time in the hospital, and the doctors had permanently disfigured Kim's arm.

With no training in the disciplined use of formal problem-solving and no sense of personal responsibility for determining the root cause, the doctors transitioned into the final phase of poor problem resolution behavior: blaming the patient. The head of psychiatry for Brigham and Women's asked to meet with us. As always, we were more than cooperative and gladly complied with the request. We were very open about Kim's entire personal history. Kim shared that she was molested by a neighbor for years as a child, that she battled through depression following the loss of our son, and that she would like to know why she is almost bleeding to death seemingly randomly. I marveled at Kim for being the strongest survivor of bad things that I had ever met. Meanwhile, the doctors were building their case to blame her with a diagnosis of Munchausen syndrome.

The bleeding started again three months after the skin graft experiment was executed. During this visit, in 2002, the doctors decided to give Kim another plasma transfusion as there was a belief that this stopped the bleeding in a prior episode. Unfortunately, they failed to use irradiated plasma, which caused Kim to have a severe allergic reaction that required resuscitation. Yes, this additional workaround could have killed her, but, fortunately, they were able to bring her back.

By this time, my confidence in my ability to use the 7-step framework and manage teams of SMEs (regardless of their area of expertise) was increasing at work every day. The best doctors in Boston were utterly at a loss for what to do next and called us in for a meeting. I started the meeting by asking what they planned on doing next. To my complete dismay, they both responded that they would run a series of factor XIII tests. At that point, it all just clicked. I replied, "Okay, neither of you are using disciplined problem-solving. I'm going to lead you through an exercise that will allow us to solve this problem in about 7 minutes. I need a whiteboard and a marker." Without saying anything, they proceeded to retrieve a rolling whiteboard with a few markers. I put my frustration and anger aside and focused on what was most important for Kim. It was time to lead SMEs through a challenging problem to get to an answer. I was confident that the framework would lead to success. I first explained how the process works. I wrote "Problem Statement" on the top of the whiteboard and then "Facts" on the left, and "Questions" on the right. I clearly defined both facts and questions and gave them a quick overview of the process we were about to use. I then began the session as follows:

Problem Statement:

- Kim periodically experiences massive internal hemorrhaging for no known reason.

And then, I proceeded to list the facts as we knew them at that time.

Facts:

- I listed documented incidents of traumatic bruises or surgery between 1989 and 2002 with their corresponding dates.

- I listed bleeding episodes and their corresponding dates.

I turned to confirm that they agreed with the facts I was listing and to see if they had any questions. These were all well-documented in Kim's binders. They agreed with the list. I then indicated that I was going to do some simple math. Math, after all, can be considered an undeniable fact.

Facts, Continued:

- The bleeding episodes occurred two and a half to three months after surgery or other major trauma.

At this point, I moved to the right side of the board, the question side. I looked back at the doctors and said, "Look, I don't care what happens in the first month, like clotting, because that is not what the facts are leading me to question." I turned back to the whiteboard and wrote the following:

Question:

- What happens in the third month of the bleeding process?

I then turned back to them and asked them to please answer the question. I received the following response: "In the third month of the bleeding process, you need to dissolve the clot. Failure to dissolve the clot could lead to blocked arteries, a stroke, or a heart attack." In more than thirteen years of dealing with this issue, this response was the first time anyone mentioned the word "dissolving." We were only a few minutes into the discussion. "Perfect," I said. I erased everything and documented the new facts.

New Facts:

- Dissolving a clot occurs in the second and third months.

- Kim has massive bleeding in the third month of the bleeding process.

I then wrote what I thought were several obvious questions on the right side of the board.

New Questions:

- What proteins or enzymes are used in or produced by the dissolving process?

- What are the proper human levels for these proteins or enzymes?

- What are Kim's levels compared to the norms for these levels?

I again turned to them to ask for the answer to each of these questions. They indicated that tissue plasminogen activator (tPA) and plasminogen activator inhibitor (PAI-1) were critical for the dissolving process to work. The activator is the clot dissolver, while the inhibitor is a control to ensure that the clot dissolves slowly. They went on to say that testing for these levels is very challenging since they only exist if you are in the process of dissolving a clot; during previous clot treatments, they didn't think to test Kim's tPA or PAI-1 levels. They added, however, that they thought we should now contact another SME, a genetic hematologist from the University of Michigan. We benefited from the coincidence that this specialist interned with the doctors in Boston, so they were familiar with his work. As mentioned previously, it is your responsibility to position the team to identify and exploit coincidences of knowledge and luck as the problem resolution leader. After thirteen years of absolutely no learning and no progress, this entire discussion took less than 7 minutes.

We still had to chase more detail before we could hope to find a resolution. In particular, we still did not know if the issue was progressive and whether or not a treatment existed. Kim reached out to the specialist in Michigan and forwarded the numerous three-ring binders of information.

Shortly before leaving for Michigan, we obtained all of Kim's detailed medical records. While driving, we reviewed the comprehensive psychiatry report. The document shed light on the depths of blame that we were unaware of previously. The report read, in summary, "Nice couple. Intelligent. Very open, sincere, and concerned. At this point, I believe this is a physiological problem that needs to be pursued. However, if nothing physiological is found within one year perhaps a case of folie à deux should be considered." The report explained that this is a French psychiatric term that translates to "double madness" and that Kim and I might be in on this together. Our motivation could be to get back at the medical profession for failing to recognize that we were losing our son during Kim's pregnancy. We could be causing the bleeding by using drugs obtained from my father, a retired pharmacist happily spending his days golfing in Florida. We saw, in writing, that doctors were attempting to blame Kim for the bleeding episodes rather than focusing on simple, disciplined problem-solving. This effort to blame Kim for all of her medical problems over the years was the worst example of blame culture gone wrong that I have ever seen.

Fortunately, to our welcome surprise, the doctor in Michigan, easily the most intelligent person I will ever meet, clearly practiced disciplined problem-solving. His diligence instilled tremendous confidence in us even after everything we had been through before this visit. He started with a question.

Question:

- Kim, you said your ancestors were from Germany. Did they come directly to the U.S. from Germany?

Kim responded with the following fact:

Fact:

- Kim's ancestors migrated from Germany to Switzerland and then, ultimately, to the U.S.

Kim's information led to the doctor's next question.

New Question:

- Do you know where they lived in
  Switzerland?

Unfortunately, that information was not readily available so he stood up and pulled down a map of Switzerland. The map had a small red circle around one region. "Your relatives lived here, in Tamins, Switzerland, and they were likely either Amish or Mennonite," he stated confidently. We were both expressionless and confused. We didn't know if this doctor was mad or brilliant. He went on to introduce a few more critical facts.

New Facts:

- Kim's maiden name is an extremely common
  Mennonite name in Tamins.

- He first discovered a PAI-1 deficiency in an
  Amish girl seven years before our meeting.
  The disorder, at that point, was only known
  to exist in the Amish and Mennonites.

- The gene that controls PAI-1 is the SERPINE1 gene. The mutation of this gene traces back to the town of Tamins, Switzerland.

And Then All of the Dots
Were Connected

As we have since learned, Kim's ancestors were prominent members of the Mennonite community in Tamins before migrating to the U.S. and converting their religion. Kim is one of the only non-Amish people in the world to have a PAI-1 deficiency. He explained that there was a medication, Amicar, that he could prescribe that would control any future bleeding episodes. Amicar is used every day in hospitals to control bleeding and clotting during heart surgery.

He sat down and continued, "I think I can explain everything that's ever happened to you, medically speaking." He reviewed Cody's autopsy and informed us that there is no data on the effects of a PAI-1 deficiency on pregnancy, but he knew what it was supposed to do during pregnancy. PAI-1 controls how quickly the placenta breaks down in the same way that it controls how a clot breaks down. It makes logical sense to assume that a failure to control how fast the placenta dissolves could result in the placenta being prematurely calcified. This condition would fail to provide the nutrition required to sustain life and produce the unfortunate result that we experienced. He added that the only thing he could not explain was how we had two perfectly healthy, beautiful daughters. He said that we should appreciate those two miracles every day, which we do.

We were finally in possession of a prescription as a result of what we learned from a 7-minute whiteboard exercise! As of 2021, Kim required doses of Amicar a few times, and each time, it stopped any problems. As I write this, Kim is a very healthy fifty-seven-year-old mom of two beautiful adult daughters, leading a normal, healthy life working as a middle school math teacher. No one embraces the importance of a problem-solving framework more than Kim.

Chapter 8

Conclusion

Would you use the Solved In 7 framework if you were managing the operations of a nuclear power plant? I was recently discussing the framework with a fellow practitioner, Karen, who is an operations manager in a nuclear power plant. Karen was made aware of an escalating situation relating to flow valves. The team indicated that there was excessive vibration in a number of critical water pipes. The team mentioned that they believed they knew what was causing the issue, but they would have to enter the restricted area to obtain more information. The area in question contains asbestos and, as such, requires special protective clothing with forty-eight pounds of apparatus for each individual. Karen was concerned that the team was chasing an untested theory and potentially placing the team at unnecessary risk before properly following a problem-solving process. Karen asked everyone to stand down so they could focus on documenting the known facts and questions immediately. The team listed a few key facts and gauge readings. The readings indicated increased vibration but did not shed light on the actual cause. Karen had a number of questions about the narrow focus of the information provided and asked the team to include gauge readings from further upstream and downstream before proceeding. Karen wanted to ensure that they were considering all available facts so as to avoid being focused on one theory.

Once all of the gauge readings were listed, the team performed an assessment on the full spectrum of readings to see if any new, important information was revealed through comparison. An anomaly, previously not discussed, was identified. It was upstream from the perceived problem and, without going into the technical details, was causing the increased vibration and prevalence of asbestos dust downstream. The team was then able to resolve the problem prior to entering the restricted area to perform cleanup activities. Had they entered the room as originally planned, they would not have been able to resolve the problem and would only have placed themselves at unnecessary risk. With the problem resolved, the team quickly performed the necessary, correctly focused cleanup activities.

Imagine what could have happened in each of the stories in this book if the problem *hadn't* been solved. What would the outcome be? What might happen in your life if the biggest problem you're facing never gets solved efficiently?

The ineffective behaviors discussed in this book are natural human instincts. They do not make you a bad person, but they will block your ability to solve your most challenging personal and professional problems consistently and efficiently. For corporations, employees will continue to implement workarounds rather than solve underlying problems. Workarounds will increase risk and decrease efficiency. A culture of blame will continue to fester, and high-performing employees who are not able to flourish in such an environment will depart. Product launches will be delayed and market share will erode as a result of time lost while employees chase unsupported theories and incorrect problem statements. People you know, and possibly yourself, will suffer from misdiagnoses or delayed diagnoses, often resulting in death, simply because no one was trained to utilize a problem-solving framework. Consider if these are behaviors you can accept in yourself, your colleagues, your team, your children's teachers, and, most importantly, those responsible for your healthcare.

Doing better simply requires the disciplined use of the Solved In 7 framework, which I introduced in Chapter 2. Let's review its 7 steps:

1. Form the team.

2. Train the team.

3. State the problem clearly.

4. Document the known facts.

5. Document the existing questions.

6. Assign questions to the experts and document the new facts that are learned.

7. Review the new facts as a team and repeat the process from Step 3 until the root cause is learned. Always edit and restate the problem statement based on what has been newly learned.

Chapter 2 also introduced the four common behaviors that are witnessed when a proven framework is not used. The four inefficient, risky practices include:

1. Avoidance via workaround

2. Stuck on a theory

3. Stuck on blame

4. Stuck on the wrong problem

The next four chapters provided compelling and relatable stories to demonstrate the applicability of the framework in both professional and personal situations. These chapters also provided key insights that will allow you to recognize each of these behaviors. Chapter 3 featured an example where an operations team developed and implemented a workaround that decreased efficiency and increased risk rather than solving the underlying problem in a matter of minutes. This chapter also presented a personal situation in which a homeowner implemented a workaround that shifted the inconvenience of his problem to a different impact rather than taking a few minutes to solve the underlying issue.

Chapter 4 dealt with the concept of being stuck on a theory. This behavior was demonstrated in the example of two software developers who were convinced that they had introduced a defect. A quick exercise based on the Solved In 7 framework determined that the issue was actually due to a defect from a vendor tool that was assumed to have been working correctly. This chapter also introduced the first use of the framework to resolve a medical issue. You learned, in this chapter, that you can resolve challenging problems despite having little to no subject matter expertise. You don't necessarily need to be a doctor to solve challenging medical issues. You will instead be a problem-solving leader guiding the technical experts through the learning process.

In Chapter 5, you learned how the blame approach develops in situations where there is no clear ownership of the problem resolution. You saw technologists blame users for an implementation failure, and you saw teachers blame a student for dyslexia. This chapter also discussed the negative impact of a culture of blame on employee turnover, as well as the impact on morale of a failure to solve underlying problems quickly as accusations begin to fly.

In Chapter 6, you read about being stuck on the wrong

problem. It is common, if not inevitable, to begin the process with the wrong problem statement. As you follow the Solved In 7 framework, you will reassess the problem statement as you go and inevitably modify it. Failure to modify the problem statement will hinder the learning process. This was evident in the workplace issue where a team was convinced that something in the system had been broken, and they were determined to figure out who broke it, when, in fact, the system executed exactly as designed. The results were unexpected because of a control flag problem that occurred earlier that evening; they were chasing the wrong problem. The same was true for the personal scenario in which the parents were convinced that their child was telling mistruths because of another child's bad influence in her life. In fact, the actual problem was a lack of trust between all parties. Again, this chapter also provides evidence of the negative impact on human relationships and interactions when problems are not addressed with a disciplined approach such as the Solved In 7 framework.

Finally, in Chapter 7, you witnessed all four of the ineffective behaviors. You read that the failure to use a framework delayed the proper diagnosis of a rare bleeding disorder for thirteen years at a cost of millions of dollars and the permanent disfigurement of a patient who, at one point, had to be resuscitated as the result of an ill-advised treatment. You saw that when someone with no medical background assumed the role of problem-solving leader, using the Solved In 7 framework, the doctors were guided to the proper diagnosis in 7 minutes.

Is your average time to solve problems less than 7 minutes? Are your employees working collaboratively with a proper framework to resolve problems so they can focus the majority of their time on being productive, creative, and innovative? Are the numerous professionals in your personal life taking responsibility for every problem, including medical issues? You can and should demand better. The Solved In 7 framework empowers you to do exactly that.

Use the framework on a problem you've already resolved. Define the problem as you initially understood it along with the facts and questions as they were known at the start. Iterate through the process until you are comfortable with it. Try it on a new problem. Keep using it until it becomes second nature. You will not be disappointed. You will also be better prepared to serve as a healthcare advocate if you are ever required to do so, which I hope you are not.

If this is not something you are comfortable doing yourself, or if you are looking for someone to train your teams, you may contact us at SolvedIn7.com. We offer interactive training classes (in person or virtual) that run roughly two hours. If you have challenging professional issues or personal medical issues, we offer consulting services to guide your experts through the learning process or to coach you through the leadership role. You may also contact us regarding consulting services via SolvedIn7.com.

The greatest reward I take away from this book, and the primary reason I set out to write it, is helping others bring order to chaos. I love hearing problem-solving success stories. Please share yours in implementing the framework via SolvedIn7.com.

Acknowledgments

There are many cherished family, friends, and associates who have helped me along the journey of writing this book:

My wife and best friend, Kim Sholler, inspired me to always focus on moving forward and survive regardless of the cards that are dealt.

My oldest daughter, Jessie, inspired me to be creative and chase my passion.

My youngest daughter, Courtney, offered great, honest feedback and served as a sounding board throughout the writing journey.

My sister, Andrea, provided iterations upon iterations of outstanding feedback throughout the writing process.

My parents, Ruthe and Lloyd, gave me a lifetime of unwavering support and led by example. Thank you!

My brother, Bob, taught me to remain calm and act decisively when headlights are coming straight at you.

My mother-in-law, Marilyn, and sister- and brothers-in-law, Dawn, Mark, and Mike, offered their own excellent feedback and different perspectives.

Shane Herrell also provided excellent feedback and connected me to critical resources for the completion of this book.

Linda Kroger gave me her own well-thought-out feedback.

Kelley O'Brien offered feedback with her usual attention to detail that is second to none.

Liz Danforth, who I had not communicated with since childhood, nonetheless provided timely and important feedback.

Michael Silvermintz was invaluable for being straightforward and saying what he was thinking.

Fidelity Investments placed a premium on disciplined problem-solving and supported my professional growth for twenty-seven years.

I value Dr. David Ginsburg for being brilliant and respectful of patients.

I admire and appreciate Peggy Barrett for being the most empathetic person ever born.

Stan Drake was the first person to ask me to "do that thing I do" to solve a complex technical problem.

Debbie Nicklaus was the first person to excitedly track me down to share that she used the framework to solve a challenging problem.

Taylor Roberts was the first non-Fidelity person to hire me for problem-solving training.

Appendix

SOLVEDin7

Solved in 7

Seven-Step Framework

STEP ONE	**Establish the Team**	1 to 3 experts
STEP TWO	**Train the Team**	1 to 3 minutes
STEP THREE	**State the Problem**	1 sentence

STEP FOUR — List Facts

- Verifiable information only
- Confirm statements attributed to others
- Take nothing for granted

STEP FIVE — List Questions

- List theories as questions
- List all questions
- Listen carefully for follow-up questions

STEP SIX — Assign Questions to Experts and Record New Facts

- Assign in parallel
- Record newly learned facts in real time
- Reinforce adherence to the framework

STEP SEVEN — Repeat

© Copyright 2022, Solved in 7 LLC. All Rights Reserved.

About the Author

Jim Sholler is the founder of Solved In 7, a company that offers problem-resolution services for any obstacle, no matter how intractable it might seem. Prior to founding Solved In 7, Jim worked for Fidelity Investments for twenty-seven years across many disciplines, including computer operations, software delivery, service management, and, of course, the help desk.

Jim built his brand as "The Fixer" on his lifelong commitment to disciplined problem-solving. A graduate of the Columbia University School of Engineering and the NYU Stern School of Business, Jim now lives in North Carolina with his wife, Kim. Connect with him at SolvedIn7.com.

CPSIA information can be obtained
at www.ICGtesting.com
Printed in the USA
JSHW031102070522
25625JS00001B/37